a year in the life of the bowland fells andy stansfield

a year in the life of the bowland fells andy stansfield

FRANCES LINCOLN LIMITED
PUBLISHERS

Frances Lincoln Ltd
4 Torriano Mews
Torriano Avenue
London NW5 2RZ
www.franceslincoln.com

A Year in the Life of the Bowland Fells
Copyright © Frances Lincoln Limited 2011
Text and photographs copyright © Andy Stansfield 2011
First Frances Lincoln edition 2011

British Library Cataloguing-in-Publication data
A catalogue record for this book is available from the
British Library.

ISBN: 978-0-7112-3220-4

Printed and bound in China

9 8 7 6 5 4 3 2 1

A lone sheep watches the sunrise above
Austwick Common on the eastern fringe of
the fells to the north of Gisburn Forest.

contents

map

introduction

The images and descriptions on the pages which follow represent a continuing personal exploration of one of the author's favourite locations which, with the completion of this work, has now given rise to three books. Yet, despite having travelled the length and breadth of the UK during the last five decades, exploring many parts of it in minute detail, the Forest of Bowland continues to be as alluring as ever. Every visit reveals something new. A chat with a local farmer here, swapping notes with a fellow bird watcher there, pausing for a moment to look more closely at the landscape at a different time of day from any previous visit to the same location...the outcome is always the same: renewed wonder at just how beautiful this precious landscape is.

Before preparation was even contemplated it was necessary to determine the focus of the work which would follow, so the decision was made to concentrate on the centre of that broadly defined area called the Forest of Bowland. There is only one definitive area which bears the name, and that is the 312 square miles of the Forest of Bowland Area of Outstanding Natural Beauty. However, the AONB includes huge swathes of agricultural land which surround the real heart of the area, much of which comprises the Bowland Fells Site of Special Scientific Interest and that has an area of only 61 square miles. So what follows is a very subjective journey, lasting

Several roads through the area provide easy access to spectacular scenery. This road winds its way down from Cross of Greet, with Grey Crag and the screes of White Greet on the right.

LEFT: There are several roads which traverse the area at a moderately high altitude relative to the fell tops, providing easier access to great walking, like this route over Waddington Fell.

almost exactly twelve months, through a unique upland landscape.

Unique is a powerful word, and one which is not used lightly. Despite the fact that the area as a whole is well served by minor roads, there is still a central massif which provides a substantial and largely unbroken wilderness at an altitude of 300 metres (984 feet) or more. This provides a moorland habitat, fringed by rushy pasture, which is ideal for a wide range of birds of prey but which is home to one in particular: the hen harrier. The Bowland fells are the only moorland habitat in England which is used on a regular and ongoing basis by breeding hen harriers, one of which is used as the symbol for the AONB. With only 15 breeding females in the country, that alone makes Bowland not just unique but vitally important.

Balancing ecological systems with public access and recreational opportunities in Bowland, which is recognised as being internationally important for a wide range of flora and fauna, is far from easy. Nevertheless, the AONB was the first legally protected region in

The Lancashire Cycleway passes through the area and ardent road cyclists are frequently seen, such as this one near to completing the climb over Bowland Knotts.

Access roads in winter can be closed, or at least extremely treacherous, but there are always determined and experienced drivers who will brave the challenging conditions.

RIGHT: The weather can change quickly on the fells, with cloud and rain sweeping in off Morecambe Bay in minutes. It is always wise to prepare for the worst when out for the day, as shelter is in short supply once you are above 300 metres.

England to be awarded the European Charter for Sustainable Tourism in Protected Areas. The fells and upland dales serve north-west England as a destination for three activities in particular: walking and bird watching, often combined, and cycling. The Lancashire Cycleway, popular for those with road bikes, traverses the area and Gisburn Forest provides a variety of routes for off-road cycling – the neighbouring Yorkshire Dales being a better bet for bridleways and green roads.

Despite the fact that the Bowland fells don't have the altitude of those in the Lake District, the highest being only 531 metres (1,742 feet) above sea level, the area has to be taken seriously by fell walkers because of the terrain, the relative lack of visitors and therefore the sense of isolation, and the weather systems rolling in off Morecambe Bay. For the most part, the fells offer very little shelter, apart from occasional 'luncheon huts' marked on the Ordnance Survey map which serve the grouse shooting fraternity for a few days each year. Tree cover is largely non-existent, apart from sparse clough woodlands and the occasional plantation – clough being the local name for a gully on the fell side. In fact, first time visitors to the area often question the use of the term 'forest' at all, but the term is used in the medieval sense of a hunting reserve, which is exactly what it used to be. Like much of England, a large proportion of the ancient woodland which once covered the area has all but disappeared.

Access to Bowland's wilder places is invariably by car, unfortunately. Although a limited bus service is also maintained, this is not cost-effective and is subject to the ups and downs of funding so there is little point in being specific here, other than to say that current and almost certainly future services originate in Clitheroe and Garstang. Facilities such as car parking, toilets and cafes are few and far between and largely restricted to the few small villages serving the fells, Slaidburn and Dunsop Bridge in particular – so the old maxim 'pack it in, pack it out' usually applies.

Finally, if this book is your introduction to Bowland, it is hoped that the images it contains do justice to the variety of scenery on offer and that they entice you to visit again and again. If you already know and love the area, hopefully these pages will encourage you, like the author, to make your exploration of its small wonders a lifelong journey.

While the fell tops can be saturated, there are few pools or small tarns to create additional obstacles, so few in fact that they are rarely named. This one was captured very early in the morning bathed in soft light, its still surface mirroring a crisp blue sky and the crags beyond.

RIGHT: While the colours can be bland in winter and early spring, a sunny day with blue sky makes all the difference.

Sunset over the central fells in mid-
November proves that the Forest of
Bowland isn't necessarily drab in winter.

spring

Spring arrives fashionably late, with little regard for the dates on the calendar with its clichéd images of daffodils and bluebells. Where there is shelter and the watery sun can filter through, the first signs of new growth can be found in miniature, if you look closely enough. But as for the panoramic sweep of fells above 300 metres (984 feet), the rough grasses will remain bleached of colour and still in the raw grip of a numbing wind off Morecambe Bay for another month. Ground-nesting birds are faced with finding nest sites which they hope are safe from predation and human interference, accidental or otherwise, as well as being sheltered from the occasional icy blast which remains a real threat long into May. And hope is the dominant mood for the three-season hill-walker too, the previous summer now a distant memory, eager to embrace new routes and a new year.

Attractive heart-shaped leaves of wood sorrel emerge through pine needles at the base of a tree. Wood sorrel, with its delicately veined white flowers, is known as an indicator of ancient woodland.

It's April Fool's Day but the weather is no joke, as a biting wind sweeps off Morecambe Bay and a thin covering of fresh snow is deposited on Wolf Fell, seen here from the Jeffrey Hill end of Longridge Fell.

RIGHT: (Top) Buds are just about brave enough to make an appearance in the last week of April, possibly deterred by the presence of a Christmas tree beneath them, a lasting reminder of how tough winter and early spring have been.
(Bottom) Side-lighting from the watery afternoon sun brings out the grey tones of Lower Fence Wood on Whitemore Knot, with just a hint of colour and the promise of foliage to come.

The tarn on Beacon Fell still shows little sign
of spring but within a few weeks the dragonfly
and damselfly nymphs will complete their
metamorphosis, crawling out of the peaty
water up plant stems to finally take to the wing.

Still draped with last autumn's fallen leaves, a largely rotten tree stump in Gisburn Forest manages to provide support for new growth in April. Spring arrives later and later as you gain height onto the fells.

Lots of first-time visitors to the Forest of Bowland ask for directions to the Forest when faced with scenes like this, without understanding that the term is used in the medieval sense, meaning a hunting reserve.

The lower slopes of Abbeystead Fell, dappled with sunshine and cloud shadow, overlook the way into the area from the west.

Habitation in and around the fells is generally restricted to isolated cottages and farms, all of which lie below the 300m contour.

The area between Stocks Reservoir (out of shot on the right) and the central fells to the left is gentle and varied in character, a mixture of grazing land and young plantations. The huge estate of water supplier United Utilities is managed from its base nearby on the shores of the reservoir.

Hawthornthwaite Fell, still showing signs of heather burning the previous autumn, and an unnamed tarn which is one of the author's favourite stopping-off points for a spot of curlew watching on the way into the western fells.

BELOW: In the distance Ingleborough, one of Yorkshire's Three Peaks, rises behind the shadowed fells above Catlow Plantation, through which the oddly named stream of Kearsden Holes flows before feeding the River Hodder.

The tree-clad top of Birkett Fell in the distance peeps out
over the shoulder of New Laund Hill, nearest the camera
and known for its 'fairy holes', the two hills straddling the
River Hodder to the south of Dunsop Bridge.

The bright new foliage of early May, an unmistakeable shade of green for the first fortnight as all landscape photographers know, is in stark contrast to the muted rough grassland at the foot of Hawthornthwaite Fell.

Sphagnum moss acts like a sponge, drawing water from the peat below and giving it a rich green colour, in stark contrast to the lifeless grasses and dried out heather around it.

LEFT: (Top) The green hairstreak butterfly, the only green one in Britain, may even be seen high up the fell sides, its distinctive wings looking almost phosphorescent one moment and flat matt green the next.
(Top right) Pussy willow, also known as goat willow or sallow, produces two types of catkins depending on sex. The male, shown here near Beacon Fell Tarn, produces striking yellow catkins, but those of the female plant are longer, more silky and green.
(Bottom) A green-veined white butterfly photographed near Cross of Greet Bridge, the underside of its wings displaying its characteristic markings for the camera.

freedom to roam

The Countryside and Rights of Way Act 2000 (CRoW) was instrumental in drastically improving the public's right to explore open countryside on foot, making a significant difference to the access of Bowland's grouse moors in particular. It is easy to take heather moorland for granted in the UK, but 75% of the world's upland heather moorland can be found within our shores, as well as 15% of the planet's blanket bog. While the area's grouse moors have become relatively derestricted, there are still many legal protection measures in place to conserve these important habitats. It is also important to appreciate that, while the CRoW Act extends pedestrian access it does not permit the collection of rock samples or plants, the lighting of fires, swimming, nor wild camping except in Scotland, and on designated Access Land there may be localised restrictions at certain times of the year, particularly with regard to dogs.

Almost all of the central uplands of Bowland are subject to protective legislation in one form or another. The entire area falls within the Forest of Bowland Area of Outstanding Natural Beauty, designated under the same legislation as National Parks. In addition, the 61.8 square miles of the Bowland Fells SSSI (Site of Special Scientific Interest) accounts for much of the area covered by this book. Some SSSIs have an extra layer of European protective legislation, leading them to be additionally designated as Special Protection Areas (SPAs), and the Bowland Fells SSSI is one of these. Special Protection Areas are locations within the European Union deemed to be of international importance for the breeding, wintering or passing migration of rare and vulnerable species of bird. In short, the Bowland fells are very much part of the natural equivalent of the crown jewels, so the ability (though not the right) to access their slopes should carry with it some degree of reverence.

In many areas it is now possible to make use of tracks which have been created by the landowners for a variety of purposes, maintenance in the case of United Utilities or access to shooting locations on the

Islands of root-bound peat, known as 'hags', can be relatively small like this one on Cabin Flat, a metre wide and almost as high, or they can be quite extensive. These can present obstacles to following a compass bearing in foul weather, added to which they are invariably surrounded by a sea of glutinous and slippery peat in wet weather.

LEFT: Waddington Fell in early summer is easily accessed from the car park on its summit.

Abbeystead and Duchy of Lancaster Estates. Some make for easy walking. Others are badly rutted, stony and are regularly scoured by run-off after heavy rain, making them a challenge even for the 4WD vehicles of estate workers, or others with access such as employees of Natural England or scientists occasionally conducting local studies. In practice, you will rarely come across any of these vehicles but from time to time major maintenance programmes have to be fitted in and require vehicular access – though helicopters are also used in remote areas for dropping in necessary materials. For example, United Utilities have recently carried out extensive fencing work in the Langden valley, are constantly engaged in replanting clough woodlands, and frequently have to strengthen river banks which are in danger of collapse. These tracks offer a quicker and easier way into otherwise wild countryside and it is easy, once initial access has been gained, for the walker to leave these more popular routes behind in favour of greater solitude.

LEFT: (Top) There is an extensive network of footpaths criss-crossing Bowland, though bridleways are less plentiful than in the adjoining Yorkshire Dales, making life a little more difficult for horse riders and off-road cyclists.
(Middle) This track is easy to navigate on otherwise featureless terrain, but among the heather of the fell tops following what appears on the map as a distinctive path isn't always quite so straightforward.
(Bottom) Footpath erosion is an issue in places, despite the relatively low number of visitors to the area.
(Bottom Right) The Bowland fells are a working environment and it is essential to follow the Country Code. Dog owners in particular should acquaint themselves with localised Access Land restrictions.

RIGHT: Walkers make the steady climb westwards across Lingy Pits Breast, beyond Langden Castle and opposite moody Fiendsdale. Ahead lie Weasel Clough, Raven Scar and Dead Man's Stake Clough. Such names do not guarantee that you will be rewarded with sightings of weasels or ravens – or dead men for that matter.

The most popular of these access tracks is undoubtedly the one along Langden Brook, accessed from between the village of Dunsop Bridge and the Trough of Bowland, where there is parking for around 20 cars while a butty van operates daily for much of the year. This route is especially popular with bird watchers and is used for RSPB guided walks. Just down the road lies the less popular but equally interesting starting point of Hareden, from which a very rough track runs along Hareden Brook, parallel to Langden Brook and leading to equally desolate fells where both hen harriers and eagle owls have recently bred. There is some room to park at Hareden too, and a very pleasant bridleway starts here and runs between 344m (1,129ft) high Mellor Knoll and the much more substantial 496m (1,677ft) high bulk of Totridge before passing through the woods of Whitemore, eventually emerging on the road south west from Burholme Bridge.

For the less hardy, the less ambulant or those with younger children who want to savour the flavour of the area's sweeping landscapes for nothing more than a stroll or a picnic, there is no finer place to go than the north-west corner of Bowland. Between the exposed gritstone of Clougha and Caton wind farm lie Artle Dale and Littledale which are attractive enough, but an offshoot of Littledale Road will lead you immediately south of the wind farm towards west Roeburndale with fine views over Mallowdale Pike and the old salt road over Salter Fell. Before you get to Winder Farm there is an area of Access Land on the left which is easily explored via a track which isn't marked on OS maps. The public road ends just short of Winder Farm, from which a level but muddy path follows the upper contours of the east side of Claughton Moor parallel to Roeburndale below. Hen harrier, merlin and peregrine falcon can be seen in this area if you are fortunate.

Roeburndale (west) is reached from Caton, but continue round to Wray and you will see a signpost to Roeburndale (east), the River Roeburn being straddled by these two unconnected roads. The eastern version also peters out, in this case at High Salter Farm – the highest of three, the other two being Low Salter and Middle Salter. It is from High Salter that the rough Hornby Road heads south onto the fell tops, an old salt road now a by-way favoured by occasional off-road motorcyclists who, to be fair, are usually equally mature in years and riding habits. South of Salter Fell, where the track crosses Croasdale Fell, its route coincides with a former Roman road. This ancient track is the longest single route in Bowland, heading due south east for almost its entire length to just short of Slaidburn with barely a meander in sight, making navigation easy enough. Nevertheless, it is a challenge because of its isolation and the complete lack of shelter from the wind and rain which are no strangers here.

The issue of navigation is a real cause for concern. Bowland is close to the coast and the weather can shift dramatically inside an hour.

While the vast majority of fell walkers encountered are adequately clothed, provisioned, and carrying a map when they set out for the day, there is always a small but significant proportion that are not. There are two main reasons for this. Firstly, there are those who are deceived by both apparent good weather and the easy start to walks at locations where there is provision for parking, plus the beginning of the route is one of those wide and gentle access routes for estate vehicles referred to above.

Secondly, there those who do not carry a map, and in this terrain it really needs to be a 1:25,000 series OS map. The most worrying are those who think they can simply rely on a mobile phone to summon assistance should it be necessary, because network coverage in the area is to all intents and purposes non-existent. Then there are those who carry what can become a soggy and illegible A4 print out from the internet of the route they intend to follow, which becomes completely irrelevant when they stray from it. Finally, there are those who rely exclusively on a handheld GPS unit – these are an invaluable aid but are of most value in this type of landscape when used in conjunction with a map. The 1:25,000 series OS map not only provides additional fine detail but the mere fact that it covers a wide area means that you can use distant features to help pinpoint your location. That can be a vital factor when the immediate terrain is largely featureless, which can be the case in substantial parts of these fells.

If you believe the author is scaremongering, talk to members of the Bowland Pennine Mountain Rescue Team, or even to Andrew

The wind farm on Caton Moor is a landmark nobody can miss when entering the area from Lancaster, Quernmore or Caton.

LEFT: This inviting track – not even marked on the 1:25,000 Ordnance Survey map – leads onto a large pocket of rarely-visited access land north of Littledale and west of Roeburndale. A planning application for 20 wind turbines on this Access Land was recently refused, though a revised application for just 13 is now under consideration.

and Adele Wilson who operate the 'butty van' on the Trough road by Langden Brook. They will tell you of parties who have 'arrived' late in the day and been dismayed to learn that they are eight or ten miles from their intended destination! Andrew has been kind enough to ferry people in his car back to their real destination on many occasions. (Incidentally, if you're looking for sustenance in the area, there are also cafes at the Post Office in Dunsop Bridge and by the car park and toilets in Slaidburn.)

Of course, calculated risk is part of thrill of the outdoors, for those who are experienced enough to make such judgements, and there are organised events on the Bowland Fells which necessitate the involvement of the mountain rescue team as a precautionary measure. Such events include organised walks involving large numbers of people, fell races, and the Bowland Challenge event. This is a weekend team competition requiring fell walking and navigational skills which takes place every summer, though the 2010 event had to be cancelled due to circumstances beyond the organisers' control.

Teams of from two to six adults have to visit as many specified grid references as possible within a ten hour timeframe. The teams camp on Friday and Saturday nights, with a meal provided both evenings, and on the Friday evening are issued maps and a list of up to 100 grid

references, with varying numbers of points allocated to each. They then while away the evening planning how, between them, they can amass the greatest number of points. An outline route plan, which incorporates the mid-point control check common to every team, must be submitted before departure on the Saturday. Random checks are carried out to ensure that all participants are suitably dressed and carry the list of mandatory items for each individual or the team as a whole. Bearing in mind that the Bowland Challenge usually attracts only the fittest and most experienced participants, that they are working as a team in an environment where similarly experienced people are doing likewise, and that they are all supported by the mountain rescue team safety net, it just serves to emphasise the naivety of the some of those ill-prepared walkers described earlier who set off without a care in the world until it all goes horribly wrong.

The CRoW Act does allow farmers and landowners the discretion to suspend or restrict access for 28 days each year, for any reason. In addition, they may apply for long-term restrictions or closures in the interests of land management, safety or fire prevention. Details of any

Two adequately clothed fell walkers approach Shooters Pile on their way up Grit Fell.

RIGHT: There is one very good reason for taking a 1:25,000 scale ($2^1/_2$ miles to 1 inch) Ordnance Survey map out with you in preference to a 1:50,000 edition: it includes field boundaries like this dry stone wall, even on the fell tops where there are no fields. When bad weather moves in suddenly, provided you already know where you are in relation to the features around you and can pinpoint that on the map, such details can save you from getting completely lost. The trick is to always know where you are, not blindly put miles on the clock and only consider your position when it is too late.

The 430m trig point above the spring of Knottend Well, looking south west over the Hodder valley toward Lamb Hill Farm and Saddle Hill at 6.45am, with early morning mist still lingering in the distance.

closures or restrictions should be indicated by signs. One example of such restrictions places a requirement on dog owners to keep their dog on a lead of no longer than two metres between March 1 and July 31 (the breeding season for ground-nesting birds) and all year when near livestock. In some areas of grouse moor, dogs may be excluded entirely.

It is always necessary to acknowledge that even the fells are a working environment and that people's livelihoods depend on your cooperation. When you encounter those who work the land, the depth of background information they can reveal during a casual chat can increase your enjoyment and appreciation of the landscape enormously, so take a breather when the opportunity arises and make time to converse with those you meet.

RIGHT: (Top) There are plenty of opportunities for walking in hot weather without the need to carry waterproofs, extra food, first aid kit and spare clothing. But all these should be considered essential if venturing into Bowland's wilderness areas at any time of the year, as the weather can be fickle and you cannot guarantee to meet other walkers if you get into difficulties.

(Middle) One of the best places to take a young family for an easy nature walk is Beacon Fell Country Park, where a variety of short routes are available taking in a wide range of different settings and habitats. There is also an educational display, a cafe and toilets, so all needs are catered for.

(Bottom) Responsible dog owners like these are a welcome sight, but their freedom to roam can still be restricted to protect ground nesting birds and livestock on Access Land.

summer

Summer means a visual feast of rich greens, brightly coloured caterpillars and butterflies, blue skies reflected in trickling streams and the deep red hues of dawn. But it is also a time to close your eyes and take in the sounds of the fells: the strange whistles of sika deer in Gisburn Forest cutting the crisp pre-dawn air, the alarm calls of red grouse ringing out as you tread the dew-laden moorland as the sun slowly warms your back. High above, circling buzzards emit their plaintive mewing call and chuckling kestrels hover at lesser altitudes above unwitting prey. And then there is the silence that comes with solitude. Even in the summer, on high days and holidays, the Bowland fells can be surprisingly empty places and it is not uncommon to walk all day, drinking in the sights and sounds of this wild place, without meeting a soul.

The slopes of Catlow Fell, from the pines bordering White Syke Clough, and a rowan tree festooned with berries in the foreground, perhaps an omen of another bad winter to come.

Soft light at dawn on the northern fells, with the
distinctive summit of Ingleborough rising out of the
early morning mist which shrouds both villages of
High and Low Bentham in the valley below.

A grey day along the Dunsop valley, this is
a popular walk with bird watchers – not least
because it leads to the hunting ground of the
first pair of eagle owls to take up residence
in the area.

The small plantation in the background accounts for most of the tree cover above Tagglesmire, on the crest between Bradford Fell and Easington Fell, but there is also a scattering of isolated pines which are visually fascinating at the western end of the plantation.

A sense of space is heightened on a balmy summer's day by wide skies and the simple lines of the landscape on New Laund Hill.

The view across upper Roeburndale towards Haylot Farm and Haylot Fell, seen from near High Salter on the old 'salt road'– a rough track known as Hornby Road which traverses Salter Fell and joins the Roman road over Croasdale Fell in the direction of Slaidburn.

The River Dunsop and the summit of Middle
Knoll, the latter filling the space at the top of this
Y-shaped valley.

One of the greenest and gentlest fell tops, Mellor Knoll fits in well with the tranquillity of the Hodder valley between Dunsop Bridge and Whitewell. Just beyond it, to the north and west, the fells suddenly take on their full upland character.

BELOW: The view north from the start of an attractive bridleway which starts a mile south west of Burholme Bridge heading northwards to Hareden on the Trough road.

Longridge Fell: the widening Hodder valley separates
this ridge from the central fells and it is often ignored in
favour of them. Yet it retains a similar landscape character,
is easier to access, and provides dramatic views of the
central massif as well as of Pendle to the east.

The southern side of Bowland is undoubtedly the most pastoral aspect of the area, with broad valleys gradually giving way to gentle fells whose lower slopes sport plantations or small patches of broad-leaved woodland, the latter often occupying cloughs running down the fell sides.

An isolated barn on Tatham Fells, on the north side of the central massif, with views westwards across farmland to Goodber Common.

Far from being colourless, cameo views on the fells can be stunning, such as this image captured close to the Trough of Bowland itself. In the year this book was being prepared, however, the heather put on a very much shorter display than is usually the case.

RIGHT: The River Hodder starts life beneath Catlow Fell,
draining into Stocks Reservoir before following its meandering
course through the villages of Slaidburn, Newton and Dunsop
Bridge to join the River Ribble south of Clitheroe.

The River Hodder at Cross of Greet bridge with Bowland Knotts
in the distance. The remains of the actual Cross of Greet lie at
the top of the pass above the bridge, but only the base remains
at the roadside and it is easily missed.

RIGHT: Compared with areas like the Lake District, cairns are not found very frequently but there is a series of them, of which this is one, east of Clougha on the route over Grit Fell to Ward's Stone.

The view eastwards toward Ward's Stone from Cabin Flat: this is the same part of the fell which is being deliberately burned to regenerate the heather in the centre of the image on page 77.

the crags

The central fells are comprised of hard sandstone called Millstone Grit, which was laid down approximately 300 million years ago during the Carboniferous period. It is typical of many sedimentary rocks dating from this time, created from compressed sand, plants and the organic remains of marine creatures which populated the shallow sea covering the area. Eventually the sea level dropped and the landmass was left exposed, to be eroded first by the weather and later by the huge ice sheet which covered northern Britain until 10,000 years ago. It was this glacial ice sheet, its meltwaters and the act of its northward withdrawal, which scoured the folded layers of sedimentary rock to produce the fells and valleys we see today,

including the line of exposed gritstone outcrops which runs across the area in an east/west configuration.

The fact that sandstone erodes relatively easily, even the tougher grit formations like these, has led to the soft rounded profiles of many of the fells. Add to this the thick layers of peat which can be up to ten feet deep, blanket bog, sphagnum moss and coarse grassland, heather and bracken and it is no surprise that most panoramic views show a skyline with little in the way of sharply defined crags and ridges, such as the frequent 'scars' found only a few miles away in the classic limestone scenery of the Yorkshire Dales. The most visible exceptions from a distance are in the west at Clougha and the north

LEFT: The most westerly crags are found on the Access Land of Clougha, rising here above the gorse and bracken. On a clear day an ascent of Clougha rewards the walker with a panorama incorporating views over another former medieval hunting estate, Quernmore, and of Morecambe Bay and the Lake District.

The distinct line of rock outcrops straddling Bowland Knotts, shown here in the immediate foreground, can easily be seen in this view south eastwards towards Knotteranum and Whelp Stone Crag, the latter rising above the most northerly stretch of Gisburn Forest.

Looking south over Old Moss and Cat Knot early in the day from a height of only 430m (1,411ft), blessed with excellent visibility, the view from this unnamed crag was superb and well worth the effort of rising early.

The crags between Knottend Well and Crutchenber Fell are seen reflected in this unnamed tarn.

east in the form of several extensive craggy outcrops which lie either side of the road over Bowland Knotts. The remainder can be found mostly on the central plateau or its southern slopes.

Bowland Knotts lies on the road northwards from Slaidburn, via Stocks Reservoir and Gisburn Forest, to the twin villages of High and Low Bentham. At this point, where the road reaches one of the highest passes in the whole of Bowland, there is a little off-road parking which enables easy access to crags to both east and west. The line of crags, outcrops and glacial debris immediately to the west of Bowland Knotts runs for about 600 yards culminating with a trig point at an altitude of 430m (1,411ft) and a 360° view that takes in the Three Peaks to the north and widening Hodder valley to the south. Immediately below to the south west lies Cross of Greet Bridge, on the only other road northwards in the eastern fells, which climbs past Catlow Fell to the remains of the Cross of Greet itself at another pass, but one which is surrounded on all sides by uninviting featureless moor.

The crags across Bowland are often only discernible from lower down by picking out the less smooth lines of the horizon, clearly seen here above Catlow Plantation and Hasgill Fell.

To the east and south east of Bowland Knotts lies a series of outcrops forming well defined and named crags over a much greater distance. The first of these is Knotteranum and the most distant is Whelp Stone Crag. The latter is just over two miles from Bowland Knotts, as the crow flies, and lies on the eastern edge of Gisburn Forest. It is much more easily accessed from its eastern flank, but also lies on the longest of the marked cycle routes through Gisburn Forest from the Cocklet Hill car park.

Between this series of crags in the east and Clougha in the west lie a number of other places where the gritty rock cap of Bowland lies exposed, particularly the swathe of central fells which includes Wolfhole Crag and Ward's Stone, at 561m (1,840ft) the highest point in the whole of Bowland. Both of these lie on a path which traverses the relatively flat plateau on a west-east line, but off this line lie a number of scattered crags, such as Haresyke Crag and the inevitable Long Crag – the latter name being applied to several different locations –

Thorn Crag, on the skyline towards the right, can be reached easily from Tarnbrook by taking the path which passes the small aqueduct on the left of the photo. This is a quicker route than using the shooting track up to Long Crag, as described on page 70, then traversing west.

LEFT: This stile, on the west side of which one has to negotiate this jumble of rock detritus, can be found on the path leading from the Access Land of Clougha eastwards to Ward's Stone and Wolfhole Crag. Ascending the stile affords one of the finest 360° panoramas in the whole of the north-west of England.

on the Black Side of Tarnbrook Fell. A shooting track from the hamlet of Tarnbrook leads directly up to Long Crag and nearby Hell Crag. A short distance west of this and of huge interest to climbers lies Thorn Crag, a popular bouldering venue which includes what has been described as 'possibly the hardest route on gritstone' first climbed by John Gaskins who named the climb 'A Moment of Clarity'. There is an excellent pdf guide to Thorn Crag's routes from Greg Chapman, complete with photos, which can be downloaded free from http:// blog.rockrun.com/thorn-crag-mini-guide.html.

Another name found in several locations is Hanging Stone. This may appear just as a non-specific Hanging Stone, as is the case of the one on the east side of the road at Bowland Knotts, or the location may be specific, such as Whitendale Hanging Stones. These weather-sculpted rocks can be found half way between Wolfhole Crag and Whitendale, overlooking the exact geographic centre of the UK

With a little imagination, it wouldn't be difficult to assign the names of animals to some of the outcrops, such as this one which appears to have a definite 'face' to it.

There aren't that many 'true' crags, but areas of ground level outcrop have been included in the subject matter, such as this on the west side of Grit Fell. Beyond the dry stone wall lie the tops of the Yorkshire Dales.

as calculated by Ordnance Survey, taking into account all 401 of the UK's islands.

Extensive ground-level outcrops may not qualify as crags but they have been formed and revealed through the same processes and provide significant visual interest in the landscape as a whole, especially where the upland plateau tends to be largely devoid of other natural features. In places these appear not dissimilar to the limestone pavement of the adjoining Yorkshire Dales, displaying the same clint and gryke structure which has been emphasised by weathering. Such outcrops appear as a layer of blocks which are usually adorned by the smaller birds which frequent the fell tops, such as the attractive wheatear.

These blocks of sedimentary rock tend to split along the bedding planes and some, despite their enormous weight, have been tossed aside by retreating glaciers and left in a precariously balanced jumble,

now encrusted with lichen, at the foot of some of these outcrops, adding significantly to the visual impact these crags create along the horizon.

But one of the most fascinating sights is that of the combination of nature's handiwork and man's ability to integrate it into the art of dry stone walling. There are countless locations where stone walls seem to blend with outcrops in places which must have severely challenged the ingenuity of the craftsmen due to the topography. When you add to this scene the deep weathering scars which some of these rocks bear, the combined effect is no less than a work of art.

In places the crags are surrounded by clusters of huge boulders, some of which were left delicately balanced by retreating ice some 10,000 years ago.

RIGHT: Clear evidence of weathering can be seen here, slightly acidic rainwater having helped to scour these remarkable grooves in the gritstone.

autumn

In many ways, autumn is the most vibrant of the seasons with the rich green bracken turning to rust and the crisp blue skies which follow the passing of a weather front replacing the more moisture-laden air of the summer months. The birch trees of the cloughs and higher reaches of Gisburn Forest turn gold and occasional vivid green strips of limed pasture brighten the patchwork of the fell sides. On damp and shadowed woodland floors mushrooms and toadstools flourish. The sounds of rutting deer permeate the dawn, perhaps more welcome to the ears than the crack of a shotgun as another red grouse is collected by the soft palate of a springer spaniel. But shooting is part of the Bowland life cycle too and the late autumn sight of smoke billowing across the deliberately fired heather reminds us of the need for regeneration in the months to come.

Moorland, larch woodland and bracken, together with a ditch which lies out of sight just beyond the bracken, combine to provide a variety of inter-linked habitats in a small area: the rich bio-diversity of the Bowland fells is internationally recognised.

Beyond this solitary barn at Brunton Laithe, a mile west of Stocks Reservoir, patches of orange and brown on the distant fells show that early autumn has arrived.

Moorland fires are always a danger at this time of year, but the ones captured here near Ward's Stone have been ignited deliberately so that the heather is rejuvenated for the benefit of the red grouse population.

RIGHT: The vivid colours in this image of the Trough of Bowland, the pass over which the infamous Pendle Witches were transported to Lancaster for trial in 1612, shows the area at its most benign.

The River Roeburn drains the northern fells, flowing northwards through the village of Wray. Roeburndale is cut deep into the fell sides and provides a lush contrast to the barren sweep of moorland on either side. Here a single frond in a thick swathe of bracken bordering the river decides that autumn is at hand.

The identification of mushrooms and toadstools is a difficult business, with some 914 varieties and a further 3,000 larger fungi in the British Isles. This was found on larch woodland floor and resembles the death cap, the most deadly variety known and for which there is no known antidote. Of course, it could also be harmless, but would you want to take the risk?

Littledale and the lower slopes of Haylot Fell from the north, bathed in soft late-afternoon light. The mixture of moorland, rough pasture with rushes, and numerous patches of woodland and plantation make the area popular with discerning bird watchers.

Carved by streams after heavy rain, winding gullies such as this – often completely dry in the summer months – provide localised pockets of trees on bare fell sides. These gullies are called 'cloughs' and are important habitats for a variety of small mammals and birds, also attracting raptors in search of prey.

RIGHT: (Top) The foliage starts to change colour in this copse, below the crag known as Holdron Castle, situated on the south facing slopes of the valley drained by Langden Brook. This is a popular route for birdwatching walks, including bird of prey identification walks guided by the RSPB.
(Bottom Left) The remarkable contortions of the chanterelle mushroom make an unusual sight, captured here beneath pines in Gisburn Forest. It is edible, apparently with a slightly peppery taste and a fragrance resembling apricots, but – as with all mushrooms – should never be eaten unless doubly certain of its identity.
(Bottom Right) Among the dew laden grass and fallen leaves, spiders create elaborate and delicate webs which attract moisture as well as prey and shine like strings of minute pearls in the morning sun.

One of the author's favourite images of the area, this scene captures both the gentle and dramatic sides of Bowland's character. The dark fell side demands to be taken seriously, in stark contrast with the inviting blue ribbon of Langden Brook winding its way gently eastward.

LEFT: The view northwards from Cross of Greet bridge on a glorious autumn day makes this quiet spot a place to linger.

Mallowdale Pike and Mallow Gill, viewed from the north-west.
In the foreground on the right of the image, a pheasant shoot is
taking place. Half a dozen people with shotguns are just visible,
with the beaters out of shot to the right. Moments before the first
shots were fired the author was watching a merlin perched on a
fence post – it didn't stay long.

a wing and a prayer

Bowland's relative isolation and wide variety of habitats make it suitable for a wide range of birds, including some of the rarest in the country, the most notable being the hen harrier. Other species are not necessarily rare but aren't seen very often except by those with sharp eyes and a spotting scope: ring ouzels frequenting the cloughs which cut the fell sides, or small and nervous woodland birds like the nuthatch. Then there are those which come as a surprise to folk who don't know a great deal about the area or birds in general, such as the large colonies, amounting to 10% of the UK population, of lesser black-backed gulls.

Farmers may apply for grants to help conserve the wading birds which frequent the rushy pastures that lie between the green valley bottoms and the coarse peaty grassland of the fell sides. They are encouraged to create small 'scrapes' by literally scraping back the surface of the land to reveal the mud and standing water so loved by waders. Retaining the rushes which are scattered across these pastures is also something requested of the farmers. The outcome is there for all visitors to see: oystercatchers, redshanks, greenshanks, lapwings and curlews are common sights, given the appropriate habitat and season, and some of these will return to the same specific pasture year after year to breed.

The problem these ground-nesting birds have is that their eggs

A great spotted woodpecker perched in the treetops of Gisburn Forest brightened up an otherwise unsuccessful dawn spent hunting, photographically speaking, the reclusive sika deer.

RIGHT: (Top) A variety of waders can regularly be seen, with oystercatchers in particular being both striking visually, often seen perched on a wall, and easy to identify by their distinctive alarm call and white wing bars when small flocks take flight. (Bottom) Lapwings are one of the most common ground-nesting birds, making their chicks especially vulnerable in the first few weeks of their lives.

LEFT: The nuthatch, one of the author's favourite small birds, can be seen in woodland across the area – if you are lucky. This bird rarely stays still for more than a fraction of a second, so photo opportunities are extremely limited.

and chicks are especially vulnerable to predators, mammals such as foxes and stoats as well as raptors. This doesn't just apply to waders either as the ground nesting birds of the heather moorland, such as the grouse and even the hen harrier, are also at risk. Given that the area supports ravens, owls, buzzards, peregrine falcons, and even the occasional visiting gyr falcon, eagle or osprey, life is a risky business for a fledgling because all these species are in competition for survival in a shared habitat. Sometimes this leads to inevitable tragedy, but it can also provide an exciting spectacle. One afternoon in late October, the author was privileged to watch a female hen harrier and a short-eared owl sparring for a full 15 minutes as they both attempted to quarter the same rushy pasture. This was at a known winter roost where, on the same day, a merlin and a great spotted woodpecker were also seen in the same habitat.

Beneath the natural drama of normal competition between

species lies a deeper darker undercurrent revolving around gamekeepers, the regal hen harrier with both its official and its self-appointed protectors, and the European eagle owl – hero or villain depending on your point of view. The key element is the importance of these fells for the incredibly precarious survival of the hen harrier in England, with Bowland being described by Stephen Murphy of Natural England's Hen Harrier Recovery Project as 'the crucible' of England's hen harrier breeding activity.

To put the hen harrier's scarcity into context, only a dozen attempts to breed were recorded in England during 2010 with a total of 61 eggs laid, just over half of which failed to produce fledged young, for a variety of reasons including predation. From the remaining 28 eggs some 23 young fledged, compared with only 15 the previous year. But these national figures don't emphasise the importance of the Bowland fells in all this. Of these dozen countrywide breeding attempts, ten were on the United Utilities Bowland Estate though

The distinctive barn owl will be found all year round, hunting small mammals around farms, barns and adjacent fields. It is usually nocturnal but will also hunt during the daytime when feeding its young.

RIGHT: (Top) The distinctive beak and alarm call of the curlew also make it immediately recognisable. In late spring it can often be found flying back and forth between rough grassland and nearby pastures, with peak numbers approaching 3,000 pairs across Bowland. (Far Right) One ground-nesting bird that didn't survive predation. Although birds and their eggs may fall prey to larger species, crows as well as raptors, they are also at risk from foxes and stoats. (Bottom) A brace of red-legged partridges on rough ground to the east of Caton Moor. Traditionally, these birds are resident in the south and east of the country and their movement north may prove to be yet another indicator of climate change, along with stonechat numbers which have risen markedly during the last decade.

only five of these were successful, producing 13 new birds. A sixth nest on adjoining land produced a further five young from the six eggs laid. (The final productive nest was in Cumbria, from which five chicks fledged.) Sadly, this was what could be viewed as a successful year after 2009's even lower tally – but that was not a good year for voles either and these form part of the hen harrier's staple diet, along with smaller birds such as the meadow pipit.

Despite successful breeding, and layers of legal protection combined with intense study and monitoring, the hen harrier population does not appear to be growing as it should. Mortality rates during the first winter are a particular concern. Temporary rises in population occur due to large numbers of birds visiting from Scotland and northern Europe, swelling communal winter roost numbers for a short time to as many as 20 in a given roost, and UK numbers including Scotland to as high as 750, with perhaps 200 in England alone. Bowland's adult hen harriers may also migrate southwards for the winter, but the juveniles tend to head into the Pennines as the most immediate means of extending their foraging area. Young females and some males leave their natal area in August, usually after a few exploratory trips, before establishing themselves in a new roost area around which they forage to a radius of five miles or so.

Some males travel considerable distances during autumn. One has been recorded as travelling from Bowland to Wiltshire where it spent around ten days, making a brief excursion to the south coast before flying back to Bowland at the beginning of November. Stopping off briefly in Shropshire on its return journey, it completed a round trip of 625 miles in a fortnight. But the most dramatic record being logged, as preparation of this book nears completion, is of an adult male which left its natal area in the Scottish Borders on 15 September to arrive in northern Spain on 13 October. En route it was recorded briefly near the towns of Aberystwyth and Plymouth, spending a fortnight in Brittany until 12 October, then flying 300 miles in 24 hours over the Bay of Biscay to arrive at the Cantabrian coast on 13 October.

The monitoring of such movement is largely down to the satellite tagging of harrier chicks which enables their later movements to be tracked with some accuracy. But some of these birds, quite literally, fall off the radar. Stephen Murphy of Natural England, who has been using this technology for several years, knows exactly where some of these birds fall. In one year the satellite signals from no fewer than six of Bowland's tagged hen harriers disappeared while over grouse moorland in the North Pennines, almost certainly due to the birds being shot. In a separate twelve-month period three birds were lost, this time in a very precise area, which may ultimately help the

ABOVE: (Top) Stephen Murphy of Natural England tagging a hen harrier chick.
Photo courtesy of David Sowter.
(Bottom) Hen harrier chicks immediately prior to being satellite-tagged. Their age is important to the day as each tag is made to fit exactly.
Photo courtesy of David Sowter.

Commonly seen in small localised flocks across the fells and surrounding pastures, though hard to identify precisely in flight, the meadow pipit often falls prey to the hen harrier.

Percentage of breeding attempts failing due to satellite-tagged adult hen harriers 'disappearing'. The dramatic failure of hen harrier breeding attempts during 2002–08 on English grouse moors other than those in Bowland is shown here. Adult hen harriers are hardly ever predated by larger raptors so these statics point to deliberate persecution. (Source: Natural England)

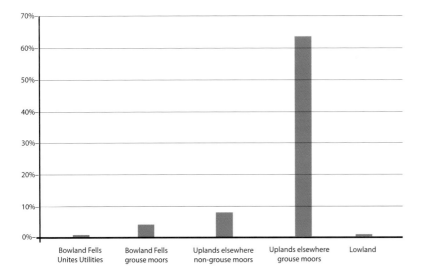

Natural England Hen Harrier Recovery Project and police Wildlife Crime Officers to narrow their focus in an attempt to bring culprits to justice.

Much of central Bowland is comprised of three large estates owned by the Duchy of Lancaster (effectively The Queen), the trustees of The Grosvenor Estate of whom the 6th Duke of Westminster is the chairman, and the water provider United Utilities. Each estate employs a number of people to whom it falls to conserve and protect wildlife on its properties, in conjunction with national bodies like Natural England and the RSPB and mindful of European legislation and designated Sites of Special Scientific Interest and Special Protection Areas.

Where grouse shooting is a vital source of income, gamekeepers are expected to perform a balancing act between protecting the grouse, at least until the 'glorious 12th' of August, and conserving endangered species like the hen harrier. The latter is obviously protected by the Wildlife and Countryside Act 1981, but accusations of shooting or poisoning, or interfering with their nests, are regularly levelled at gamekeepers in general. This sad state of affairs, with all gamekeepers being tarred with the same brush, will continue until the guilty few are prosecuted. None of this was helped by a high profile but unsuccessful police investigation into the alleged shooting of two hen harriers on the royal estate at Sandringham in 2007. Both birds were seen by witnesses to fall from the sky at the same time as shots were fired, but the proverbial smoking gun was never found and neither were the dead birds, so no one was brought to account.

The Wildlife and Countryside Act 1981 applies solely to wild animals and not to those bred in captivity. This is one of several issues with regard to the eagle owls, which are generally assumed to be escapees that were bred in captivity, or the young of such, though these birds are also known to visit these shores from the European mainland. But who would want to keep an eagle owl in captivity, apart from an owl rescue centre? In fact, the Department for Environment, Food and Rural Affairs (DEFRA) estimate that around 3,000 eagle owls are kept in captivity in the UK and history tells us that a significant number of owners would find the bird too much of a handful and release it into the countryside.

The same legislation also prohibits the release of non-native species into the wild and one of the major arguments which continues to rage is whether or not the eagle owl is or is not native to our shores. Although there are historical records referencing the eagle owl, none is deemed to contain sufficient description to confirm that the sighting was indeed that species. The British Ornithologists' Union

Records Committee added the bird to the official UK list of species in 1975. But, following a review of nearly 100 supposed sightings between 1684 and the late 19th century, it was later removed from the list in 1996. That same year a well-documented pair on MoD land in North Yorkshire raised three young and went on to successfully rear around 20 during the following decade. It is highly likely that some of these colonised the Bowland fells, the north eastern edge of which is actually in the white rose county.

The pair of eagle owls in Whitendale, a couple of miles north of Dunsop Bridge, bred successfully during 2007 and three young were reared. From the start, these birds raised concerns about their possible predatory habits. Known to favour rabbits as prey in the countryside, escaped birds in built up areas have been known to take small dogs too. Cautious optimism held sway for a time among those concerned about the eagle owls' potential impact on other wildlife in

ABOVE: With the female weighing up to three kilos and with a wingspan of up to two metres, the European eagle owl presents a fearsome sight. The Forest of Bowland currently has at least three pairs with the Whitendale pair having received the greatest publicity, getting their 15 minutes of fame in the national press due to the aggressive protection of their territory.

LEFT: (Top) Female hen harrier in flight.
Photo courtesy of Richard Saunders.

(Bottom) The Whitendale eagle owls were responsible for the closure of a public footpath due to the danger of them attacking members of the public, especially those walking dogs.

the area, but it didn't take long for them to become infamous rather than celebrities. The tenant farmer at Whitendale was attacked by one of the birds while with his dog, walking along the public footpath which runs alongside the beck flowing through this deep dead-end dale cut into the central fells. This stretch of the dale was being used for both roosting and hunting by the eagle owls.

Further reports of harassment followed, especially by those walking their dogs, and the unusual step of closing the public footpath for reasons of public safety was taken by Lancashire County Council in conjunction with the police Wildlife Crime Officer for the area, PC Duncan Thomas. This story got into the national press and its impact has been so great that, three years later, the author still regularly meets people who have driven to the area solely to see the eagle owls, though many haven't a clue where to look. Nevertheless, the infamy of these birds has probably done more to publicise Bowland than anything else since spring 2007.

Eagle owls were sighted in Bowland as far back as 1985, with sightings since on the increase: numerous times in Roeburndale and along Langden Brook, as well as the well-documented pair breeding up the Dunsop valley in Whitendale. In 2010 eagle owls also bred in two further locations, with a single abandoned egg found at a nest site on the Abbeystead Estate and three owlets raised in Hareden. Although clearly favouring relatively remote parts of the area, they are obviously not deterred by much, including mankind.

Knowledge of the eating habits of these huge birds, the female of which can weigh up to three kilos and have a wingspan of up to two metres, has increased significantly during this period. Closer examination of eagle owl droppings by those actively involved in hen harrier conservation has also revealed just how widespread the eagle owl's diet can be, including finds such as the complete skull, with intact beak, of a snipe – quite a mouthful by any standards. Their inclination to prey on competing raptors is doubted by many, though a video camera, specially placed to monitor one of the hen harrier nesting sites, recorded an eagle owl attacking the parent harrier and later standing in the nest, dwarfing the eggs by its feet. The parent harrier deserted those eggs as a consequence of this interference and the nest failed.

Sightings of hen harriers are relatively scarce unless you are fortunate or, like many ardent bird watchers, you know exactly where to go and at what time of day. The best chances of seeing one are when their aerial activity is geographically restricted by two things: the raising of young, or their tendency to use specific winter roost sites. Information on the location of both is closely protected for obvious reasons. Added to which, the hen harrier is one of nearly 80 bird species listed under Schedule 1 of the Wildlife and Countryside Act, making it illegal to 'intentionally or recklessly disturb' dependent young or an adult bird while nest building, at a nest site, or while feeding its young.

Male and female hen harriers look very different: the male is pale grey with a white breast whereas the female is brown with a banded tail and tell-tale white rump. Males also tend to disperse more widely from their natal area and forage at a greater range of altitudes, whereas females tend to stay much closer to home. Male hen harriers in England tend to be largely monogamous, though that is not the case further afield. There are currently around 20 breeding females across the country, excluding winter visitors, of which 15 can be found in Bowland – if you are lucky.

Hen harrier nests are subject to much close scrutiny from a number of people who have to apply to Natural England for Scientific Licenses to monitor and inspect nest sites, and to ring or satellite-tag the fledgling harriers, as is the case for all Schedule 1 species. Additionally, raptor workers visiting United Utilities land are required to sign up to a field protocol and, if necessary, to apply for a vehicle access permit to specific locations. Although subject to less intensive scrutiny than the nests, winter roost sites are also monitored by teams of volunteers on a regular basis. If you were unintentionally in danger of disturbing one of these sites, someone would very likely be around to warn you.

These volunteers perform a vital role in hen harrier protection, but that very dedication can also lead to passionate debate, if not angry argument, about what is best for these beautiful birds. The independent and lively website www.raptorpolitics.com takes an aggressive stance in championing the cause of the hen harrier and lays the blame for its precarious existence firmly at the door of the grouse moor owners and their gamekeepers, citing nothing less than intentional persecution, as does Natural England.

All in all, there is much to pray for, not least the common sense of those whose decisions affect the very existence of some of our rarest birds, whether they are native to our country, passing migrants, or vagrants in need of assimilation into our legal framework and ecological management strategies. Despite calls for a cull of eagle owls where they are a possible threat to endangered species, the author would argue that there is a place for both the eagle owl and the hen harrier in our wilderness areas – provided the latter is left in peace to breed and its persecutors are seen to be caught and punished.

winter

The winter landscape is muted, its contours and sounds softened by snow, the weak sun barely able to put in an appearance where the topography obstructs its low trajectory. Tree shapes merge, sinuous broadleaved silhouettes blending with pines, while the snow-draped hummocks of moss beneath them just catch the light to create a miniature landscape in their own right. Widespread snow cover is rare but when it does occur all our memories of greens and purples are banished, replaced by eye-tingling brightness as open landscapes take on a different perspective. Distance is harder to judge and the fells appear temptingly benign on a blue sky day. The landscape itself, though, has a deeper longer memory of times when ancient forest clad the fells and cloughs, when deer and boar roamed freely and were hunted for sport by kings and nobles. At best today, luck will bring forth the footprints of a deer, crisply etched in the snow.

At 1.00pm in early January the winter sun barely gets above the horizon, reflecting brightly off the stream in the foreground but only providing just enough light to pick out the undulating ground beneath these trees.

Accumulations of snow turn a scattering of rocks and clumps of grass into a miniature landscape in its own right.

RIGHT: (Top) The distinctive shape of Parlick from the west, at 432m (1,417ft) the most southerly summit of note among Bowland's fells. It is a popular venue for both paragliding and full-blown gliders, the latter flying from their own airfield just out of shot on the right.

(Bottom) This scene along the Wyre Way shows New Barn and Sawpit Wood (right) merging into Pennington Wood (left). Behind these this waymarked route cuts northwards to climb gently over to the hamlet of Tarnbrook along the fringes of the central fells.

Fantastic patterns are formed by the ice partially thawing and freezing again a few inches above the surface of the Marshaw Wyre as it trickles along beneath its winter coat.

LEFT: (Top) A view across the scattered woods of Bleasdale to Fiendsdale Head and Holme House Fell, rising to Fair Snape Fell on the right. Beyond the ridge lie some of the wildest parts of the Bowland fells.
(Bottom) Mellor Knoll rises to the west of the Hodder valley's flood plain near Dunsop Bridge, looking more grand in its winter guise compared with the image on page 51.

Winter's watery sunshine creates a lattice of shadows on the snow in this copse adjacent to Oakenclough Fell on the western fringes of Bowland.

This welcome sign at Jubilee Tower is
significant in that it invites access to the
grouse moors around Clougha which
were severely restricted prior to the CRoW
legislation.

LEFT: (Top) The woods at Stang Yule are
a favourite spot of the author's, providing
superb views of the fells rising from Bleasdale,
but just getting there was tricky enough on his
particular day.
(Bottom) In the middle distance lies
Greenside Hill beyond which, almost dead
centre, can just be seen a tiny sliver of road
which is the ascent to the Trough, with Staple
Oak Fell in the background.

Snow redefines the landscape, bringing out texture and shapes which may not be noticed otherwise. Dry stone walls acquire greater contrast, as side-lighting glints off the snow adhering to their capstones, and hedgerows and trees are admired for their intricate leafless silhouettes rather than their colour.

Fells which are almost featureless in summer present even greater navigational challenges in winter. In this scene the barely identifiable Ward's Stone ridge is etched against the clear blue sky.

LEFT: Snow caps a boulder embedded in ice which has formed intricate, almost crystalline, shapes.

Remarkably, considering the extensive snow fall, the road over the Trough remains open, providing a stunning view of the descent towards Dunsop Bridge and the towering mass of Totridge.

This shooting track makes for easy access towards
Marshaw Fell and up Black Clough, which drains
Holdren Moss northwards from Black Clough
Head. Running south from the same point lies a
completely separate Black Clough which drains
into Langden Brook.

Animal tracks are easily spotted in the snow but it also makes them harder to identify as the edges tend to crumble, unless it is extremely cold. This appears to be the hoof print of either a sika or red deer, more likely the latter given where it was found.

BELOW: The farmer's work must continue whatever the weather and is made even more difficult when snow blankets the landscape, seen here at Burholme Bridge.

Index

Acknowledgments

There are many people who have helped to make this book happen, not least those who live and work among the Bowland fells and have been generous with their friendliness and anecdotes, but some I wish to thank by name, in no particular order: Andrew and Adele Wilson for numerous mugs of tea and egg barms at their butty van at Langden Brook intake; David Sowter for permission to use his images of the satellite-tagging of hen harrier fledglings; Richard Saunders who heads Natural England's Hen Harrier Recovery Project; Stephen Murphy, also of Natural England, whose knowledge of hen harriers is truly encyclopaedic, who ferried me to some of the wild places and gave me a far greater understanding and appreciation of these wonderful birds; the Forest of Bowland AONB team; Caroline Holden at United Utilities Bowland Estate Office for her time and invaluable background information; Ian Grindy, also of United Utilities, for vehicular access to the UU Estate; Terry Lally for his company on a bitter November day at an undisclosed hen harrier roost and his tips on bird watching, just one day before completion of this labour of love. Finally, to my partner Liz who reads everything I write, devours every image I capture, and always provides constructive criticism of both.